ELLIPSIS...

KHALILAH YASMIN

For Love, Muses, & Consciousness

TABLE OF CONTENTS

el·lip·sis
əˈlipsis/
noun

1. The omission from speech or writing of a word or words that are superfluous or able to be understood from contextual clues.

2. A series of dots (typically three, such as "...") that usually indicates an intentional omission of a word, sentence, or whole section from a text without altering its original meaning.

3. ...

"Black American"

They will tell me to my face that I've transcended race when my version of Black is accepted,
Yet I'm angry, belligerent, and threatening when my skin color is why I'm rejected.

When you tell me that you don't see my color, and call me the 'Brown version' of you,
You're denying my culture, you're erasing my lineage… You see it. I know that you do.

You remind me that I'm BLACK, whenever my version of natural is met with question.
I'm BLACK, when you're uncomfortable unless I tiptoe around these harsh truths and valid lessons.

You tell me we're the same, but say that my name is too difficult for you to remember.
Named after an Arabic Queen. History you've never seen and would have returned to the sender.

Unless I straighten my hair, the playing ground isn't fair.. Because kinky hair is too strange.
Your version of natural is widely accepted and mine must be painfully changed.

When I enunciate my words and speak properly with articulation, you say, I'm talking 'White'.
Because if I speak another way, that isn't as such, I'm told it's not right.

"You're pretty, what are you mixed with?" as to imply that Black isn't enough to be seen in glory.
My skin color isn't my entire journey on this planet; it's only part of my story.

You say we're not different, but every day you make sure to remind me that I AM BLACK.
I've embraced it and I love it. By now you should not have a problem with that.

Working twice as hard to get half as far only to be labeled as angry,

If you walked a day in my skin, wearing my shoes, you'd be screaming, "Come save me!"

You cannot look at my face and say that I've transcended race when every day, this *'Earth Suit'* **still is not universally accepted.**

"Erotica City"

The strongest drug that exists for a human IS another human....

You have your needle lodged into my veins

Self inflicted and committed I'm a hostage to your chains.

GAINS... I recall no losses when my muscles are contracting.

The plus to my minus, when the souls between our eyes are interacting...

I'm trippin' obviously, st-st-stumbling over my own words, I'll be damned if I fall.

Embarrassed that my heart beats so hard that I cannot answer your call.

Addicted with only a taste, I'm a feen for your version of 'coke'-

You've got the only supply that I want, strung out on all of your 'dope'.

Smoke me back; inhale me into the depths of your lungs,

till I beg for my coffin,

your dick getting hard as the insides of my pussy, they soften...

Often.

Weekend... or not, sunlight or sundown, your rules have become my own,

Obeying your shades of grey... your orders, and the sword beside your throne.

Consciously aware of every nerve ending in my body I didn't know existed,

Your mouth like a thousand lips and tongues all of you, with each and every kiss.

No longer trust myself to make proper decisions on my own behalf,

polyamory is unfamiliar and my ego wants to laugh.

Perhaps I must wake up out of this dream, and let go of this 'Erotic City' affair,

For I am a mere citizen of this town... and you call yourself *The Mayor.*

"Millionth Moon"

You're the moon in the sky in the daytime reminding me that magic exists.

You're the water 'God' made to hydrate me.

You're my respite on land if I were a fish.

You're the drug that bears no side effects, natural and wonderfully made.

You're the full house, the jackpot, the lottery when all I had was a spade.

You're the reason cancer goes into remission with slim to none chance of return.

You're the human unscathed by the fires you walked through when they watched and said that you'd burn.

You're the last push of courage that was needed to save millions of innocent lives.

You're the gracious lover satisfied with one woman when promised one hundred wives.

You're the beam of light that shines when I'm afraid to sleep in the dark; your presence makes demons in the night disappear without a whisper, without a bark.

You're the lover and the friend
Fair-weather NEVER, consistent and loyal to a fault.

You're worthy of praise; humble with grace
it's others you often exalt.

You're the "Everything is going to be okay," and making it come true with a wish,
You're the dreamy reality in a world full of torment, you ARE pure bliss.

You're 20 more years of life when I was given 20 days.
You're accepting of every life.
No matter where they lay.

You're everything I desire
You're all that I could ever wish.

You're the millionth moon in the daytime
And you do not exist.

"Broken chords"

In love with the man that sits behind the piano.

He sings his soul in bass, alto soprano.

Ammo, his gun he shoots with no blanks,

He prays to his version of God but it's me that he thanks …

And I bid him welcome with my Adieu.

My eyes tell my secrets with each rendezvous.

Ivory & ebony upon the fingers he keys,

And the union of melody when I fall to my knees.

He grabbed me by my hips; with his instruments he effortlessly made me sing his soprano.

Farewell to the brim-hatted man, whom lived in my heart, and sat behind the piano.

"My Best Dress"

The year was **1962**.

I liked to dance, you played the guitar.
I smiled to myself and you smiled from afar.

I had snuck out with my friends for the night to hear you play.
Never told my Pa where I was going because of what he would say.

He would tell me that I didn't belong there. "It's not safe to risk your life for music. The notes are not worth it."

But the music awakened chords in my soul. I wish he had heard it.

Wearing my best dress, the only one we could afford at the time.
Ma lost her job as a maid.
Boss' husband admired brown sugar & had a wandering eye.

You and I, we met eyes on occasion with the purest intent.
You winked. I wanted to draw nearer to see what you meant.

Yet it was unsafe for my kind to be enamored with someone whose skin did not match my own.
You saw me head to the door, and you came out alone.

A love routine we looked forward to after every show's applause,
A dark alley of secret kisses, hand holding, "I love you's" and au revoirs.

Jessie's hair glowed underneath the moonlight allowing me to see myself in his smile.
When anxiety rose in my body, he whispered not to worry, and stay a while.

Suddenly from the door, the lead singer pushed through with an army behind him in tote.
"Jessie's been sneaking around with a nigger, I think we should cut her throat."

You did your best to protect me, as the glass bottle was broken on the side of the bricks.
Love overpowered by hate.
They beat you and cut me until the sight made you sick.

Wearing my best dress, the only one we could afford at the time,
you screamed, **"I LOVE HER".**
My eyes faded to black staring at the *"No Negroes allowed"* sign.

"Incipient"

Straddling the line between *friendship & love*, I'm losing my balance.
Ceremoniously, I've offered my heart wringing its blood in your chalice.

Alice, I am- in a wonderland that I never considered before.

Paralleling this world the entire time, yet I had never explored.

Your lips and your eyes upon mine have become an **insatiable addiction**.

I am too careful & conscientious to succumb to affliction.

But here I stand, heart in my hand begging for your mercy.

Please set me free from your spell if you're refusing to love me.

Place me back at the tower where no one could reach me,
Set me free of your curse
I demand that you teach me!

Your chalice is full, my blood on your breath.
This whimsical fairytale may be all I have left.

Am I convincing myself that I feel something while trying to prove to myself that I don't?

Are you using my affection to feed your ego while promising that you won't?

Straddling the line between friendship & infatuation, losing my balance.

Begging for your mercy as you **drink my blood** in your chalice.

"Horned Deity"

Delusions of self perhaps in grandeur.
Illusions of others, their manipulating manner.

Perhaps I'm not much or a planner.

Throwing caution to the wind
When met with high notes and witty banter.

Maybe I should just stop believing that this is my turn,
And my heart would not obliterate,
My soul would not burn.

But alas I'm a glutton to masochistic behavior,
Choosing a self proclaimed baphomet as my savior.

Addicted to a habit that will never fulfill me,
Found what I truly loved and I've been letting him kill me.

"911"

Self defense, 18 years later but not too late.

Come near me & I promise that death is your fate.

I refuse to be another sacrifice to Satan you made.

If only the grim reaper was willing to make a fair trade.

Praying to God as a resident from heaven released.

A fiery celebration once you return to your home among all your beasts.

A bullet on standby,
On speed dial 911.
Exhausted of your torment
May God's will be done.

Tired of the nightmares, and you popping up whenever I cross your mind.
No remorse. No guilt. Just a monster with time on his side.

Flashbacks of a girl pregnant with child covered in her own blood-
screaming for help.
You kicking her with your military boots covered in mud.

I may not have been strong enough then
But now I have a license to carry.
I've come a long way from that virgin you married.

Now here we are, I thought I'd dress for this special occasion.

Organza wedding dress, GLOCK fully loaded & Swiss Army for your
face's decoration.

I warned you that you were unwelcome & to forever stay away.

Long time no see; I'll be sure to make sure that you regret this day.

Now you're crawling away, begging for mercy like I once did first.
Aww, the shoe doesn't fit so well when the shoe was once hers.

It's my turn to hear you scream gargling blood;
This cut is for the pregnant teenager you tried to cover in mud.

Hands covered in blood, I hike up my puffy dress,
My lace garter has your final gift.

Now open up wide, and give this cold chamber a kiss.

911, I'd like to report an emergency.

The man that tried to kill me for leaving him is lying next to me.

"as·phyx·i·ate"

Falling in is easy but I haven't yet mastered the escape.

Voluntarily submitting myself to severe emotional rape.

For my own sake- I need to break my own spell.

I envision and become addicted to a false heaven built inside of a very real hell.

Convinced I know myself well,
using a mallet to break the chain.
My straightjacket awaits me as I sleep amongst the sane.

In a prison, I walked into knowing I would be trapped,
my captor laughed at my naiveté and at himself he clapped.

Seems I love poison when it's disguised as healing,
this is the last time I'll feel my heart peeling…

Layers of scar tissue, that should have built a wall,
instead allow in false suitors

Reminding me not to love at all.

Laying down broken and almost left for dead,
somehow I rise again, as if I never bled.

I'm my own enemy, addicted to a false heaven
built inside of your very real hell,
I thought I did, but I don't know myself very well.

"Seven Hundred and Fourteen"

It's been seven hundred and fourteen days since you went away.
Delusional believing I hide it well, yet think about you every. day.

It's been seven hundred and forty days since I last held you close.
Some days I think I'm going crazy…. And can feel your ghost.

Beside me… as I write this message and read it aloud forcing a smile,
I cried today for the first time in a very long while.

Reading your texts and the pictures you sent me,
I lost it on one of my last -telling you what you meant to me…

Your demons took you away from me & told you to die.
They told you I was better off…
They bamboozled you. Demons lie.

You whispered that I took your pain away…
But I guess my love dosage wasn't strong enough.. to fight.
It's been seven hundred and fourteen days since I slept through the night.

"Smoke Filled Room"

I never asked for much, a genuine friendship was enough,
But my feelings never mattered because, "I don't do that stuff."

I chose to be a loyal friend, without making you earn it.
In turn you never appreciated it, you lit and you burned it.

An opportunist in search of the next come up or joyride,
Disguising ulterior motives as sincerity, "Because I'm a nice guy"…
Riiiight.

When you lost your weight, you seemed to have also lost any good perspective.
Don't mistreat those that mean well, or you'll lose the elective.

You're feeling yourself too hard and I should have never fed your ego.
You replaced the cupcakes with compliments and now you think you're regal?

If your heart is made of shit then your physical transformation doesn't matter,
If being a dick gets your dick hard
Then your mirror is shattered.

It's getting old, don't you think? Being the thirsty dude in the comments?
Oh I'm being ridiculous because "all those bitches want it?"

Too loyal for a mutha-phucka that never gave a fuck about anyone but himself.
You want to have everything and everyone in every way…
But should go FUCK YOURSELF.

"63 minutes"

Frequently do I -believe that a love for me exists.

That somewhere beyond the broken heart is a new first kiss.

Seldom have I -experienced this,

Genuine chemistry and undeniable connection,

Throwing caution to his wind- without his protection.

Maybe if I -hadn't looked into that direction,

Been there at the same time and sat in his section,

Then I wouldn't yearn for him the way that I do,

But for 63 whole minutes I thought my wish had come true.

Crescent moon in the sky, red skirt on my hips

A stranger passed by with, "hello," on his lips.

And never have I felt such immediate bliss,

Locked in his eyes, and their eternal abyss.

Melanin in the most beautiful shade I have ever seen,

My knees buckled weak and I started to lean.

My mouth steady silent as my insides they screamed.

Pleasantly haunted by his chocolate in all of my dreams.

Hopeless romantic, caught surprised & enamored at first sight,

Fallen for a stranger before I knew his name that night.

Seldom have I- experienced this,

Never have I -felt such immediate bliss.

Crescent moon in the sky, red skirt on my hips.

A stranger passed by with, "hello," on his lips.

"Details"

In detail.

Every crevice. Each muscle before it contracted. I feel.

My imagination can bring you back from the dead and
For a millisecond that moment is real.

In detail, I can see your smile wash over the room without the intent to
wake me.

As you watched me sleep. Now; into my slumber you take me.

To a world that did not exist before your arrival.
To a fortress of magic where imagination is all necessary for my survival.

In detail, I can smell your cologne through saved voice mails on my phone.
Your laugh echoes walls you've never been.
The details of a lover I should have kept as only a friend.

"Insatiable"

(Written, recorded, and featured in the Chippendales Las Vegas show)

He's my personal statue of David.
Like a Greek God in and out of leather.
Fearless yet gentle.
He's willing to ride ….with and on me.. regardless of the weather.

I've never had it better… than the way he gives me what I need.
Training my body vigorously… and then he lets me feed…
on him… in any way he may choose

Insatiably addicted to who he makes me and how he moves.

I may not be his only but I don't even mind,
My volcano erupts as he sends a chill down my spine.

There's more to him.. than eyes will show.
You'll have to touch to see.
Some girls want love…
I just want him to fuck… me.

"Limerence"

(According to scientists, a chemical cocktail of neurotransmitters —
phenethylamine, dopamine, norepinephrine and oxytocin — are at work
when we fall for someone.)

"Find what you love and let it kill you," he said.
Lost myself in his eyes with his 'gun' to my head.
Russian roulette each time I release his trigger –
One in the chamber and one to deliver…

I figure; this love will be my death and also rebirth
He told me words have power and this is my curse.
So I rehearse and I practice, my addiction enchantment.
Walking through fire bare skinned, free of damage.

"Find what you love and let it kill you," I responded.
Handcuffed without chains, **dopamine** bondage.
In critical condition, both hands behind my back.
Stronger than any drug, heroine… I made him crack…

…My inhibitions and previous addictions
Confessions of truth are stranger than fiction.
Run away or listen to intuition that says to come close.
He killed me with his kiss- He showed me my ghost.

"Hamlet"

When it starts to hurt the most, I find myself attempting to reason with my ghost.

At times I imagine the entire planet fading to black,
I wonder if where I go, I would even want to come back.
Back to see the people and places I could not afford-
My imagination drifts to darkness & bliss.
Believe me, for I am NEVER BORED.

Yet existential anxiety plagues me,
Holding the life jacket yet no clue how to save me.

This life: GOD GAVE ME...
If there is one- I hope.
This fake ass smile does not help me cope.
There has to be more to this.
All this? Can't be it all.
So poor that my interest is simply robbing 'Peter' to pay 'Paul'.

Y'all- have no fucking clue
Of the nightmares I've lived;
The demons I've walked through.
But whom exactly am I even talking to—?
No one will see this.

They'll think it's a delayed cry for help when they read this.

But! I mean this.
I'm tired and want the life that I see in my head.

Every second I pray it comes before I am dead.

"Remember"

What if our souls collected souls of souls we have been?

And we are right now; a combination of them.

Acting out missions fulfilled over and over again,

Finding the same soul in not just this body; but that of our friends.

That feeling when you meet certain people and think, "Where have you been?"

It clicks. Lessons we didn't learn; we meet and are tested again.

Past lives are for old souls that have been here before;

Still had some unfinished business, or pined with God for "one more"…

For you this is voodoo because your soul is too new.

Spirit science is psychedelic and I must be a hippie;

I still love you even though you don't agree with me.

Loved ones we haven't seen in 1000 years…

Again we dance. Again we cheers.

Creating life in our words, our art, and every thing that we pass,

Unaware at each breath that it could be the last.
Creating passionate curiosity for the things that we've missed.
The footprints we made and the humans we've kissed.
What if our souls collected souls of souls we have been?
Do you remember now? Are you one of them?

Presses Pause

The Brain and Human Memory-

Some say that your entire life will flash before your eyes right before you die.
Others profess that you will only see the moments you love. Both instances are in relation to NDE (Near Death Experiences) and human speculation.

Is this the brain's reaction to the instant moment before it no longer interacts with the human body? The brain then into overdrive immediately floods our consciousness with every memory good or bad; whether they were frequently recalled, subconsciously buried or purposely forgotten. They're all coming back.

I imagine they're random and in no particular order; creatively making a Tarantino film out of our lives. The probability of this and a possible 100 year life being shown in mere seconds; is enough motivation to ensure the experiences, people, and places fill up the screen honorably. Time is the most magical illusion and valuable asset. NOW.

Have you thought about what you will see?

Presses Play

"Ethereal"

I can feel when I dream and when I'm awake.

If I can shake in both worlds, then which one is fake?

Or are they both realms in which we operate,

Manifesting our consciousness and our own chosen fate.

Foreshadowing further worlds-

The lives we will live and be,

Even if in this new dimension

I don't resemble eternal "me".

If this life is a dream, then what is it I am seeing when I sleep?

And if the opposite is true, which one of them is weak?

Because I know we eventually see what we speak...

We bring to life what we water,

What we feed,

What we think.

If coincidences are nothing more than timed "supposed to's..."

Then how do I distinguish the dimensional now from the deja vus?

They say anomaly of memory, call us crazy and mentally ill,

Forcing us to dumb down, deny truth, and take THEIR pill.

If I can discover truth from another being when my eyes are closed,

And see them in full,

One of these worlds is more real than the other...

And someone's feeding me bull...

Shit, maybe I'm hallucinating and both places are a dream formed beyond this dimension,

I can feel them both with the same depth, attempting to guide my intention.

Foreshadowing further worlds-
The lives we will live and be…
Look deep enough into my eyes,
You'll see ETERNAL me.

"F*CK THE APPLAUSE"

Follow me before I reach 300K

Love before it's the lie that the masses say.

See my face when I've chosen to showcase my flaws.

Beyond the selfies, the filters, the Internet faux pas.

Celebrate me because you believe in my process,
Not for false entitlement and bullshit nonsense.

Because you thought I was the shit before the television screen.

Be real when I have nothing or don't expect my loyalty.

I have the same heart that I was born with. Still learning how to filter
through bullshit.

Save the fake ass, "I always knew you would make it"

Bitch you never liked me. You don't have to fake it.

I've learned how to kiss my own ass

Flexible …
So if I choose to I can reach the yard with the perceived better grass.

Last; the place where they say the good ones finish.

In competition with myself ONLY- so guaranteed to win this.

Race; that I prefer to experience by means of genuine journey.

Not concerned with the obstacles or hurdles before me.

Like this before it's the latest trend in your news feed.

Water me without standing at my tree expecting my seed.

Remember when people took pictures with you because they genuinely
cared
Without needing your status, occupation or business to be aired.

When the news was valid and not a distracting scare tactic of sorts.
When people had a conscious whether or not they were guilty in court.

When humans did good in the world anonymously and said fuck the
applause.
Take me to a place where my skin tone isn't the stereotype for your laws.

Does it really matter if I get one million views?
Does that make my existence valid or your interest skewed?

I refuse to purposely place my tits into my selfie pic.
Even if that's the direction of superficial society
And "I am here" politics.

It doesn't matter whom I know or who knows me.

People reposting advertisements for a small fee.

Before I reach 300 K, are you here for my ass or cause I have something to say.

About the Author

Khalilah Yasmin is an author and poet. She has her Bachelor of Science in Psychology. With a keen interest in human behavior, she enjoys the dichotomy between art and psychology as a medium to alter perceptions. Yasmin currently resides in Las Vegas, Nevada.

Twitter: @KhalilahYasmin
KhalilahYasmin.com

www.ingramcontent.com/pod-product-compliance
Lightning Source LLC
Chambersburg PA
CBHW040035110426
42741CB00030B/29